06- LEBANON

Pioneer

Everything You Need to Know About

SELF-CONFIDENCE

Feeling unsure of yourself is a sign of low self-confidence.

Everything You Need to Know About

SELF-CONFIDENCE

Matthew Ignoffo, Ph.D.

THE ROSEN PUBLISHING GROUP, INC.
NEW YORK

Published in 1996, 1999 by The Rosen Publishing Group, Inc.
29 East 21st Street, New York, NY 10010

Copyright © 1999 by The Rosen Publishing Group, Inc.

Revised Edition 1999

Library of Congress Cataloging-in-Publication Data

Ignoffo, Matthew.
    Everything you need to know about self-confidence / Matthew Ignoffo.—Rev. ed.
        p.   cm.—(The need to know library)
    Includes bibliographical references and index.
    Summary: Suggests how self-confidence can be built and describes the positive effects it can have.
    ISBN 0-8239-3037-8
    1. Self-confidence—Juvenile literature. [1. Self-confidence.]
I. Title. II. Series.
BF575.S39146 1999
158'.1—dc20   95-8758
                                                         CIP
                                                         AC

Manufactured in the United States of America

Contents

Introduction

Since you've picked up this book, you're probably interested in learning more about self-confidence. The best way to begin is to look at yourself in the mirror. I don't mean a real mirror. I'm talking about the mirror of self-examination. Very few people do this because they fear that they might not like what they see. But to build your self-confidence, you have to start with the reality of who you are. As you begin to look at yourself, consider these questions:

- Do you like who you are?
- Do you believe in yourself?
- Do you think you can do the things that you want to do?
- Do you like the things that happen in your life?
- Do you feel that you have any control over your life and how others see you?
- Do you think that you are as talented and valued as other people?

People who are described as "shy," "timid," or "quiet" often have a lack of self-confidence.

If you answered no to most or all of these questions, you probably lack self-confidence. If this is the case, you are definitely not alone. Most people have some form of low self-confidence, no matter how sure of themselves they may seem.

People who lack self-confidence are often described as "shy," "timid," or "quiet." These words reflect a basic distrust of yourself that makes you doubt your abilities. You hold back from doing everything that you could do and being all that you could be.

In contrast, confident people have faith in themselves and their abilities. They strive to improve themselves and believe that they can meet life's challenges successfully.

This book shows you how to conquer your doubts about yourself and how to build your confidence. To do this you need to change the way you see yourself. As your view of yourself improves, your confidence will start to improve, too. You will begin to feel as if your whole life is getting better and that you have some control over the things you do.

After reading this book, you should be well on your way to making these changes in yourself. As you read, you may notice that many of the ideas in this book seem like simple common sense. They are! The trouble is that many people forget to use common sense. Sometimes all it takes is a reminder—like this book—to remember the importance of your instincts.

"Confidence" simply means having faith in yourself. We often lose faith in ourselves because we've had bad experiences or because we've been told things like, "You're worthless" or "You're a real loser—get a life."

If we hear these negative statements enough, we might start to talk to ourselves the same way. We might call ourselves "idiot" or "stupid" and think, "I just can't do anything right" or "I don't have what it takes." Then we might start to expect bad things to happen, and when they do, we say, "I knew that would happen. It's just the way I am."

Let me illustrate what is happening in this process. Imagine a strong wooden plank that is lying on the floor. The plank is six feet long, two feet wide, and two inches thick. If I asked you to cross the plank, you probably would have no trouble at all. But now suppose that the plank stretches between the tops of two ten-story buildings. If I asked you to cross, you would probably think I was crazy. You'd probably tell yourself, "That's too high up. If I fell, I would get killed."

You would probably refuse to cross the plank, or if you did cross it, you'd probably fall—even though you would have no trouble crossing the same plank when it was on the floor. How can we explain this difference? And what does this plank have to do with you and your confidence? Keep reading and you'll see.

For now, let me give you one hint about the meaning of the plank. Your actions and attitudes are powerfully shaped by what you choose to focus your attention on. If you look down, you will probably fall. If you look across the plank and aim your attention at the other side, you'll probably be able to get there.

The same thing is true for the way you think about yourself. When you look at yourself, what do you focus on? Do you dwell on all the negatives in your life? Do you give yourself too little credit for your achievements and successes? This book will help you turn your attention to the positive things inside and around you. And by doing this, you'll start to create even more positives in your life.

Everyone feels self-doubt at some point in their lives.

Chapter 1

Clue in to Confidence

Everyone experiences low self-confidence now and then. It happens to famous people like movie stars, astronauts, and Olympic athletes—and it can happen to you too. Losing confidence in yourself is a normal part of life. In fact, it actually serves an important purpose.

The Comfort Zone

Poor self-confidence provides a risk-free "comfort zone" where you can hide. You won't feel "comfortable" in this comfort zone, but at least you won't risk anything by staying there. This "comfort" seems easier than working to improve yourself. But something strange happens in the comfort zone—you end up using more energy staying where you are than you would use by developing your talents.

11

Malcolm's family has just moved from Florida to Vermont. Even though Malcolm was considered an excellent swimmer at his school in Florida, he is very nervous about trying out for the new school's team. As he waits to dive into the pool, his hands get very cold, and his legs start shaking. He has never felt this way about swimming before. He thinks to himself, "If I don't do well now, I won't make the team, and the guys will think I'm a loser." He walks around nervously but can't shake the chill.

When his turn comes, Malcolm might dive into the pool and swim well. But because he is so anxious, he is likely to perform as poorly as he expects. He may even decide to give up and not try out at all.

Malcolm's lack of self-confidence may also lead to difficulty in making friends. He may be so afraid of what his classmates think of him that he chooses not to introduce himself at all. Malcolm will say to himself, "I'm no better off, but I'm no worse off either. Better safe than sorry." Malcolm doesn't feel good about not making new friends, but at least he has risked nothing.

After a while, the false safety of the comfort zone starts to run your life. Eventually it can ruin your life by keeping you from becoming who you really are. Being confident, in contrast, means having faith in your true self.

How Confidence Works: Self-Talk

Poor self-confidence is manufactured. It is not your fate, even though you may think it is.

People manufacture self-confidence by using self-talk. Self-talk is simply what you tell yourself. You talk to yourself all the time, in the form of either words or feelings. At times you may feel happy, whereas at other times you may feel down or depressed. You may think, "This is really cool!" or "This stinks." You might say to yourself, "awesome!" or "bummer." All of these reactions are self-talk.

As he waits to try out for the swim team, Malcolm tells himself, "Everyone's going to think I'm a freak." As he focuses on this thought, he becomes less confident. His self-talk is so powerful that it might even lead him to perform badly or to not even try. Yet he has been an outstanding swimmer for years.

What You Think Is What You Do

A computer runs whatever program you put into it. The same thing happens inside your brain. There's a saying among computer programmers: "GIGO": Garbage in, garbage out. If you put positive information in, you get positive information out. What you are thinking is the program that influences how you act.

Corinne is a smart, well-liked high school senior. She is preparing a speech that she must give in front of the school board on why the music and art department

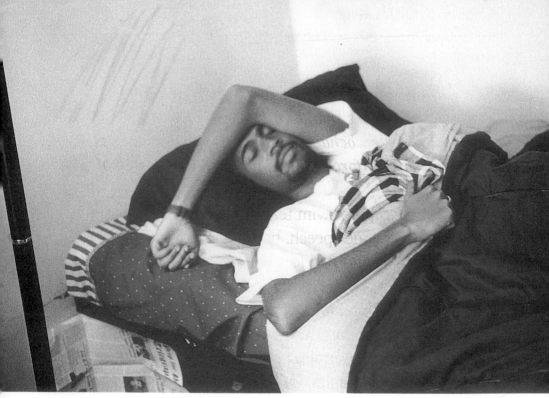

Low self-confidence can prevent you from trying anything new.

needs more funding. Even though she is a good student and a talented speaker, Corinne tells herself, "So much is riding on this. So many people are depending on me! I know I'm going to mess this up, and then we'll lose the music and art program. Everyone will blame me! I'll just freeze in front of all those people." Corinne runs this negative self-talk through her mental computer. As a result, she has difficulty rehearsing the speech and feels frightened every time she thinks of standing in front of the school board.

The problem is not that Corinne can't learn the speech and give it in an effective way. The problem is that she is causing her own defeat.

Corinne is painting a mental picture of herself

as a person who can't learn the speech and can't deliver it well. This image in her mind will determine the way she behaves. And the way she behaves will, in turn, reinforce the mental picture she has of herself.

By not risking the swim team tryout and by being scared of giving the speech, both Malcolm and Corinne are "playing it safe." They are wearing their self-image for protection and security.

But by being afraid to risk something new, they both get stuck where they are. They can't grow into the people they could become: Malcolm never tries out; Corinne freezes up. Now they have their results. They talk to themselves about the results, put that information into their computer programs, and go through the cycle again.

The Self-Fulfilling Prophecy

A common statement is, "I knew that would happen." This kind of self-talk is called the self-fulfilling prophecy. It means that what we expect to happen will happen, not because it is our fate, but because we will manufacture the results we expect.

The self-fulfilling prophecy works either for you or against you, depending on what you expect of yourself. You can put either a good program or a bad program into your mental computer. It depends on what you tell yourself and how you picture yourself. Remember: You change your level of confidence by changing your thoughts.

Chapter 2

What You Think Is What You Get

Some caution is good since it prevents us from walking off cliffs or into fires. But when caution controls you too much, you stop growing. Push back your protective mental walls to be more of who you can be. The walls are there to protect you from harm, but unless you expand the space within the walls, you stop living and become like a programmed robot.

Erroneous Thinking

We all want to avoid making mistakes. To do so, our instinct is to be cautious and follow the rules rather than being creative. But suppose a baby learning to walk tried to protect itself that way?

Fortunately, the baby doesn't use negative self-talk. The baby keeps getting up on two feet, falling down, getting up, falling down, getting up, and

People with low self-confidence often don't trust their own ability to make effective decisions.

finally taking a first step. Like the baby, at some point we have to let go of our fears.

The Poor-Confidence Cycle

You manufacture low self-confidence when you get caught in the cycle of negative self-talk. This cycle has nothing to do with things, people, or events outside of you. It has everything to do with the way you think about those things, people, or events.

There are seven types of negative self-talk that create poor self-confidence.

17

Perfectionism. If you think you have to be perfect to be acceptable, you'll never be acceptable because you'll never be perfect.

Jamal's self-talk goes like this: "I'll never be good enough to get a date with Tanisha. She wants a guy with lots of money to spend on her. She'd never even talk to me."

Tanisha is telling herself, "Jamal is so cool. It would be great to go out with hem, but he'd never ask me."

Both Jamal and Tanisha are caught in the trap. They are using "all or nothing" self-talk: "Either I'm perfect or I'm a failure." They stop themselves from talking to each other because of perfectionism.

If you were really perfect, life would be very boring. There would be nothing for you to learn or create. Be glad you aren't perfect.

Judgmental Thinking. We make negative judgments about ourselves and other people. We set such high standards that nobody can measure up to them.

Pedro would like to play the piano, but every time he practices he tells himself, "You're off the beat, stupid!" When he listens to the other band members playing, he thinks, "What a bunch of losers! We'll never play well enough to perform."

Negative judgments about ourselves and others alienate us from ourselves and even from people who might help us. As a result, we feel lonely, and loneliness makes low self-confidence worse.

Many people turn to food when they feel lonely or hopeless. Food doesn't make the problem or the feelings go away, but changing your self-talk to include positive statements can help you gain the self-confidence you need to deal with the problem head-on.

Helplessness and Hopelessness. In psychology this kind of thinking is called "external control." We see ourselves as being controlled by parents, teachers, friends, society, and life. We feel helpless and see our situation as hopeless.

Barb is ashamed because she is overweight. She tells herself, "My parents are overweight, so I inherited my fat. When I go out, I'm supposed to eat a lot just to be friendly. People would laugh if I took up jogging. I wish I could lose this fat, but I can't."

This thinking often takes the form of "I wish I could, but . . ." By indulging in it, you lock yourself into a prison of your own making.

19

Impoverished Thinking. We tell ourselves that we would feel better if we just had something that is missing in our lives.

Angela thinks, "If only I had a stereo like Corinne's, everything would be great. If only my hair were like Barb's, I'd look okay. If only I had a body like Kandace's, the guys would be attracted to me."

"If only" thinking doesn't work. Basing your ideas of yourself on the outside world can't make you confident. Confidence must come from within.

Worry. We think that if we worry enough, it will somehow help.

Nathon is running for president of the photo club. He is preparing a campaign speech. He thinks, "What if the microphone doesn't work? What if the room is too hot? What if I forget what I want to say?"

Worry involves the "What if?" trap. We imagine everything that could go wrong. Nathon thinks that by worrying, he is preparing for the speech. Actually he is making himself more nervous.

Victim Thinking. When we don't face reality and don't take responsibility for our reality, we tend to see ourselves as victims.

Kandace is considered the attractive woman at her part-time cashier job. She tells herself, "The guys all think of me as a sex object, and the women are jealous of me. I wish I weren't good-looking. I hate being afraid of my own body."

Victim thinking causes us to see reality as

Material things like clothes and hairstyles alone can't make us feel confident.

beyond our control. We feel we cannot take any responsibility for what happens to us. Pushed to the extreme, this kind of thinking causes us to hate ourselves because we seem so weak.

Self-Fulfilling Prophecy. The self-fulfilling prophecy was mentioned in Chapter 1. This kind of thinking comes from the other six types of erroneous beliefs. Notice how Jamal, Tanisha, Barb, Pedro, Angela, Nathon, and Kandace are setting themselves up to fail. They lack confidence simply because of the way they think about themselves and the world around them.

Thinking negatively about yourself may actually cause you to fail at what you're trying to do.

Recognizing the Low Self-Confidence Trap

The first step in changing yourself is to be aware of these erroneous beliefs. You have to know what the problem is before you can do anything about it. Becoming aware of what you are doing to yourself is the first step. You can build your new confidence by avoiding the negative self-talk trap.

Self-talk is like a powerful drug. It can be a harmful narcotic that destroys you and your life, or it can be penicillin that heals you and helps make you stronger.

The Power of Choice

People who have lost confidence in themselves usually believe in luck. Relying on luck to solve your problems relieves you of any sense of responsibility. But as soon as you begin to take responsibility for what happens in your life, you begin to see that things you used to attribute to luck actually are the result of choices you make.

Make the decision now to change your life by changing the way you think about yourself. This moment of decision gives you the power of choice—your choice.

Chapter 3

Knowing Yourself

To have confidence in yourself, you must know who you are and how you function.

Your Needs

Dr. William Glasser has helped many people understand themselves better so that they can create better behavior. Dr. Glasser believes that we have four needs:

The Need to Belong. We join clubs, have friends, and express our love and our desire to be loved. If we feel that we belong to nothing, love no one, and cannot find love, we are very lonely. Loneliness destroys confidence.

Malcolm felt so unsure of himself that he considered not trying out for the swim team. He felt a need to belong to the team, but his self-defeating thoughts

Joining a club or a sports team or getting a part-time job may help improve your self-confidence.

kept him from fulfilling his need. Jamal and Tanisha wanted to go out together, but they were both afraid of rejection. They felt the need to love and be loved, but their self-limiting beliefs stopped them from expressing their feelings to each other.

The Need to Achieve. Confidence exists only when we can accomplish something that we think is worthwhile. If there is nothing we feel we can do well, we view ourselves as weak. We think that there is no purpose to our lives.

Corinne wanted to save the music and art department, but she was so worried about freezing up during her speech that she was unable to rehearse it. She felt a need to achieve, but she kept sabotaging herself.

Pedro wanted to play the piano with the band, but he was so critical of himself and the others that he undermined his own talent. He felt the need to demonstrate his skill, but his self-talk held him back.

The Need for Fun. Fun comes from having something to look forward to. If we can't look forward to a better future, we feel that our lives are going nowhere.

Angela thought her life would be better if she had new material things. But she did nothing to change her view of herself, and so she remained frustrated. She felt the need for fun, but her self-defeating attitude stopped her from enjoying her life.

Malcolm wanted to fulfill his need for fun by swimming. Pedro was looking for fun by playing the piano. Jamal and Tanisha were looking for the fun they might have by getting acquainted. But all of them limited themselves by staying inside their mental prisons.

The Need for Freedom. We need to see ourselves as independent human beings. If we think of ourselves as victims of circumstances beyond our control, we lose the will to live. If we no longer feel alive, we slowly die inside.

Barb wanted to lose weight to escape what she thought was an inherited tendency to be overweight. Although she felt the need for freedom, she stopped short of achieving it by viewing herself as unable to exercise and eat sensibly.

Part of being free is recognizing that you are responsible for making your own decisions.

On the other hand, Kandace is very attractive, but she focused on the negative consequences of her appearance. She thought that men viewed her only as a sex object and that women were jealous of her. She felt the need to be free of other people's opinions, but the truth is that she *was* free of them. She just hadn't learned that it is her own thoughts that have power over her, not what other people think.

Malcolm, Jamal, Tanisha, Barb, Pedro, Angela, Corinne, Nathon, and Kandace are not aware of their needs. Therefore they have no idea that their lack of confidence stems from the fact that they are not actively fulfilling those needs. Once you are aware of your needs, you can continue growing.

Chapter 4

Making Your New Plan

I f you don't know where you are going, you'll end up someplace else.

Goals

There is an old saying, "No wind favors a ship without a destination." Imagine a ship in the middle of the ocean. If the ship has nowhere to go, the crew can't set the sails to make use of any wind. The ship just drifts. People who have no goals in life just drift.

But if the captain of the ship has a destination, he can have the crew set the sails to make use of any wind, even a wind blowing in the opposite direction. Unfortunately, many people have little idea of what they can achieve in life, and thus they aim at nothing. They feel frustrated, and their confidence is low.

Many people have a difficult time choosing a goal for themselves. This can lead to frustration and low self-confidence.

Suppose you are driving down a highway when you suddenly see a very attractive person in the lane next to you. If you shift your focus to the person in the other car, you will begin to swerve in that direction. You go where you focus your attention.

Remember the six-foot plank? If you focused on crossing the plank, you'd have no trouble. If you focused on the ten-story drop, you could easily fall. Where you send your attention is where you send yourself.

Ask yourself:

- Do I have any goals?
- How specific are they?
- What do I want to be doing a year from now?
- What do I need to do to reach my goal a year from now?
- What do I want to be doing five years from now?

If you think it is farfetched to plan ahead five years, remember, "No wind favors a ship without a destination." If you don't consider where you want to be in five years, you could just drift for five years and end up wherever the winds of life blow you. Then you will feel frustrated. That is no way to build confidence.

Look at the successful people in life. They have something most other people don't have. It's not money, cars, possessions, or big houses, although they may have all those things. They got where

Writing down your goals is the first step in achieving them.

they are because they had goals, and they kept their goals in sight all the time. They manufactured their confidence by knowing where they wanted to go, and then they did what it took to get there. Talk to some of the people in your own life whom you consider successful. Maybe they can point you in the right direction.

Changing Can't to Can

A confident person does not believe in **can't**. Suppose President John F. Kennedy had allowed **can't** to control the space program. In 1960, when he announced his goal to have an American on the moon within ten years, manned space flight was considered pure science fiction. The scientific community said it was impossible.

"Why is it impossible?" he asked. "Because we don't have the metal, the fuel, and the technology," they responded. He told them to get the metal, the fuel, and the technology. **Can't** was changed to **can**, and on July 20, 1969, the first man set foot on the moon.

Going Step by Step

When you find out the specific reasons why you **can't**, you have actually identified the ways you **can**. You know the steps that make it possible to do what you thought was impossible. Instead of viewing a seemingly impossible goal as one huge job, you break the job down into its parts and then do each part step by step.

Here are the steps in building your confidence:

Set Goals. Set specific, realistic goals that are in keeping with your talents and skills. Obviously a five-foot person would not set a goal of becoming a basketball star, but this person might set a goal of becoming an excellent coach or referee. Identify your own strengths and weaknesses when setting your goals.

- **Having a Goal Brings About the Means.**
Once you decide to do something, the means to

do it start to show up. When you decide to buy a particular make of car, suddenly you begin to see that car all over the highway and ads for it everywhere. The cars and the ads were there before, but you just didn't notice them. Now you do because you have a goal.

- **Mistakes Are Stepping-Stones.** Instead of viewing mistakes as setbacks, view them as steps toward your goal. When a baby is learning to walk, it falls down many times but just keeps on adjusting until it takes the successful first step.

- **Expect Success, Not Failure.** People who are truly confident don't focus on mistakes. They notice their successes. By keeping their focus on reaching the goal, they have the confidence to continue until the goal is achieved.

- **Trust Yourself.** A confident person has self-trust. To be confident means to have faith in yourself. If you don't trust yourself, you defeat yourself. Confident people can say, "I'm my own favorite person."

Wise Caution

We do the best we can with the self-talk and self-image that we use. So be careful what you put into your self-talk and self-image. It is wise to be cautious, but being overcautious will defeat you.

All of our behavior—including our fear and

Doing well on a test you've studied for can boost your confidence.

overcautiousness—has a positive intention: to keep us alive and happy. But sometimes people do things that can make them miserable, like taking drugs, drinking habitually, and misusing sex, because they have decided that they don't like themselves very much. They fail to realize that what they're doing is not in keeping with the goal of life and happiness. Trust yourself and focus on your positive intentions.

What Are You Doing?

Ask yourself: If I know my goals, what am I doing to achieve them? Is it working?

Sometimes people set goals but never check whether what they are doing is furthering their goals. If what you have been doing is not producing the results you want, ask yourself a very important question: What can I do differently to reach my goals?

Since you create your own behavior, you can change your behavior. You've surely heard the old saw, "If at first you don't succeed, try, try again." Let's change it to, "If at first you don't succeed, do something else." That doesn't mean that you abandon your goal. It means that you abandon the self-defeating behavior that was not moving you toward the goal.

Winners and Losers

We are all born to win. But we can create "loser" behavior that prevents us from becoming all we were meant to be. Recognizing the "loser" frame of mind can prevent you from behaving like a "loser."

Here is the way a "loser" looks at life:

- **Expects failure.**
- Feels great **anxiety** or even **panic** about life because he or she has little or no sense of control.
- **Imagines dangers and obstacles** everywhere and freezes up.
- Senses **little or no meaning or purpose** in

life and **gives up easily** when goals are not
attained.
- Has only a **vague idea of goals** and does not
really expect to attain them.

A confident person rejects such self-defeating
thoughts. A confident person uses the winner's
frame of mind:

- **Expects success.**
- Senses that he or she is **actively involved** in
life and therefore has a **sense of control** over
his or her life.
- **Uses wise caution in dealing with real
problems** and **stays in control of his or her
thoughts.**
- Senses that there is **meaning** in life and so
does not give up when goals are not attained.
- **Keeps working at attaining goals** because he
or she expects to attain them eventually.

A "loser" automatically becomes a victim. A
victim views himself or herself as an object, a
thing that is at the mercy of powerful forces
beyond his or her control. But a human being is
not designed to be an object. A human being is
meant to be a winner. A winner views himself or
herself as a responsible person.

Being responsible means being "able to
respond" or free to choose. How do you choose to
think and act?

Working toward a goal, such as eating healthier foods, can give you a sense of achievement.

Commit yourself to create do-able, realistic, positive goals, and then move toward them step by step.

Commit yourself to stop listening to your negative self-talk or the negative talk of other people. Let other people live their lives, make their choices. You are choosing a new plan and making a commitment to improve your life.

Do It Now

Now is the time to make your commitment.

Many people live in the past and keep reliving all their mistakes and negative experiences. Thus they miss the opportunity to create something new *now*. Of course you must learn from the past, but you mustn't keep thinking about it and recreating it. Move ahead and get on with your life.

Now is the only time that Malcolm can decide to try out for the swim team; that Corinne can stop worrying and start learning her speech for the school board; that Jamal and Tanisha can begin talking to each other; that Barb can start eating properly and exercising; that Pedro can acknowledge his real talent; that Angela can realize that she already has everything she needs to be happy; that Nathon can make a good speech to his club; and that Kandace can stop worrying about what other people think of her and start being herself.

What are you waiting for? *Now* is the time to set your new plan in motion.

Chapter 5

The New You

If you see yourself as a meaningless person leading a purposeless life, you will not be able to manufacture confidence.

Meaning and Purpose in Your Life

Dr. Viktor Frankl was imprisoned in a Nazi concentration camp during World War II. In his book about his experiences, *Man's Search for Meaning,* he writes that the prisoners who gave up on themselves and lost their will to live also lost any sense of meaning in their lives. They were not able to go on, and they died.

The prisoners who did not lose the will to live kept focused on the idea that their lives had purpose. No matter how sick and frail they became, they were alive when the Allied armies liberated the camps. If they could do this in a

Create a mental image of yourself enjoying success.

brutal concentration camp where they faced death every moment of every day, you can do the same no matter what you have to face in your daily life.

Many people do not like what they see when they look in a mirror. Try thinking of yourself this way: "There is only one me in all of human history. I am here for a reason. I have a talent that the world needs. If I don't develop my talent, the world will never have it. I need to become everything I was meant to be. I am here for a reason."

A self-reliant person who has self-esteem can

overcome any problems and accomplish whatever he or she needs in life. On the other hand, someone who has no self-trust, no self-worth, and therefore no reason for living, will give up at the first sign of trouble. Which kind of person will you choose to be?

Creating New Self-Talk

Replace the old, negative self-talk with new, positive self-talk that will build your self-confidence.

Positive self-talk has four qualities:

- **It's Personal.** Since your negative thoughts are about *you*, you must talk directly to yourself with your new self-talk. Use "I" in your new belief statements.

Malcolm has been telling himself, "I'll make a fool of myself if I try out for the swim team. I'll look like a rock in the water. Everyone's going to laugh." You can hear how negative he has been.

Listen to how different Malcolm sounds now: "I've been swimming since I was a little kid. I'm good at it! I can do it now. I'll show everybody what a good swimmer I am." Does this mean he will swim like an Olympic athlete? Probably not. But he's there in the pool swimming, feeling confident in his true ability.

- **It's in the Present Tense.** Use self-talk about today, not about the past or the future. The past exists only as lessons you can remember. The future, by definition, never arrives. Speak about your new goals as if they were here with you now. Use present-tense verbs.

Corinne has been telling herself, "I'll mess up this speech. I'll freeze." It's no accident that what she expects to happen does happen.

Instead, Corinne now tells herself, "I can do this. I've given lots of speeches. I've got this stuff memorized. I'm ready to give this speech!"

- **It's Positive.** You get what you focus on, so focus on what you want, not on what you don't want.

Jamal and Tanisha were both thinking, "I'm not good enough. I would never be able to say that I'd like to go out on a date. Even if I tried, I would mess up." They were focused on what they didn't want rather than on what they did want.

Their self-talk is different now: "I'm saying what I feel. I want to go out, and it's time to talk about it."

- **It's Powerful.** Do you tell yourself, "I'm an idiot! I'll never succeed! I'm a failure!"? These are strong statements. Make your new self-talk equally powerful in a positive way, showing how much fun you are having aiming at your new goals.

Keep your goal in mind as you strive to achieve it.

Barb has been telling herself, "I just can't do anything to change the fact that I've inherited a heavy body. I can't tell people that I'm trying to eat better and exercise. They'd laugh at me." These are strong statements that express weakness. We can be very powerful in sabotaging ourselves.

Barb now tells herself, "I feel totally great about deciding to lose weight. I'm excited about creating a healthy body with a fantastic good diet and awesome workouts! I love building a new body!"

Thought Reversal

Your mind cannot believe two opposite thoughts at the same time. You can short-circuit negative thoughts by replacing them with positive ones. In psychology this is called "thought reversal."

Think of the worst horror movie you ever saw. Think of how grim and scary it was. Remember every detail that you can and really concentrate on them. Notice what is happening to your thoughts and feelings as you do this.

Now erase that idea. Think of a beautiful spring day in a meadow. See the warm light of the sun on the green grass. Look at the bright colors of all the new flowers. Smell the fresh air and listen to the birds. Notice what is happening to your thoughts and feelings now.

The horror movie scene and the pleasant spring meadow exist only in your mind, but both create powerful feelings and emotions. Wherever your thoughts go, your energy goes. You can create negative energy or positive energy. It all depends on what thoughts you choose.

Be Ready for Your Doubts

In the past you've invested lots of time in making your negative self-talk come true. Don't be surprised now when the old thoughts pop up. Be ready when your mind raises doubts.

Pedro is now telling himself, "I'm jamming at

Accepting occasional self-doubt and moving on enables you to keep working toward your goal.

the keys of my piano, and the band sounds great." Nathon thinks, "I'm a strong speaker, and I'll be a shoo-in to win the election." Malcolm says to himself, "I'm a natural in the water, and I love the rush of competing." Then in the back of their minds, they hear doubts. Pedro hears, "Yeah, but suppose you're off-key." Nathon hears, "Yeah, but what if you forget part of your speech?" Malcolm hears, "Yeah, but what'll happen if you get a leg cramp in the water?"

These doubts are normal. But be ready to counter-act them so that you don't become overcautious. Tell yourself, "That's the reality. So what? Now what?"

Let's see why this three-part statement is a powerful cure for doubts:

"That's the reality." Most people lose confidence because they are afraid that something might go wrong. Telling yourself, "That's the reality" allows you to accept the truth that you are not perfect and that mistakes can happen.

"So what?" This question takes away the heavy mental burden that keeps many people worried. You accept that things may not go the way you planned. Mistakes are stepping-stones toward success.

"Now what?" This question refocuses you on the present moment. You can choose new behavior right now. Every new moment gives you the opportunity to make new choices.

And remember, change takes time. Be patient with yourself.

The Seeds of Happiness

Why is Angela frustrated when the new stereo and hairstyle don't make her happy? Because she is looking outside of herself for happiness. Happiness comes from the way you look at yourself and your life, not from things and people on the outside.

In one of the ancient Greek myths, Zeus called an emergency meeting of all the gods on Mount Olympus. He told them, "The humans have spoiled or destroyed every gift we have given them. The only thing left is this bag containing the seeds of happiness. Where can we hide this bag until humans are wise enough to make good use of the seeds?" The gods pondered the question a long time. At last they hit upon the one place where the seeds would be safe: inside the human heart.

To find happiness, you must accept yourself and become everything you are meant to be. Happiness comes from the way you think and the way you do things. It does not come from outside. It comes from within.

People lose faith in themselves because they think happiness comes from controlling other people. But the only person you can control is yourself. An old saying expresses this idea: "Change the sail, not the wind." As we navigate through life, we cannot control the wind, but we can control how we deal with the wind.

Do You Want to Be Miserable?

The misery that comes from low self-confidence allows us to play victim. When we play victim, we can manipulate other people by gaining their sympathy. We can also excuse ourselves for everything we do because, after all, we tell ourselves that we have no control over our lives.

Is this the way you want to live? Stop being miserable. Choose to rebuild your confidence now. Taking full responsibility for your life may be a bit scary at first. But it's also very exciting once you begin to see the results you can achieve.

Trying a new hobby can help you discover that you have unique skills.

Chapter 6

Aiming for Excellence

Y ou are not perfect, so you don't have to aim at perfection. Aim at excellence. When you are excellent, you make full use of your abilities and you regard yourself as a worthwhile human being. In the excellent frame of mind, you focus on the solution instead of the problem. Excellence brings quality into your life by riveting your attention on your goals instead of on any obstacles in the way.

Volunteering, joining a club, or even taking up a new hobby can be ways of getting more control over your life and gaining a sense of accomplishment.

What Is Failure?

When you aim for excellence, you realize that you cannot succeed without sometimes failing. Most people view failure as a dead end. But failure is important information in disguise. Failure tells you what not to do. The baby learning to walk fails many times, but every failure brings the baby one step closer to success.

Don't define "failure" as disaster resulting from the inability to succeed. Think of it this way:

- Failure is essential to success.
- You cannot succeed without failing often enough to discover what you need to succeed.
- Failure is the process of gathering information, adjusting your course of action, fine tuning, and focusing.
- No great success was ever achieved without all the necessary steps first being taken.
- These steps are commonly called failures.

Hitting the Bull's-Eye

The reason that many smokers lose confidence when they try to quit smoking is that they "fail" the first time, and so they give up. Actually people who do quit smoking "fail" six or seven times before they finally reach their goal. Wealthy people usually "fail" ten or twenty times in various businesses before they reach success.

Giving up after a few "failures" is like trying to hit a bull's-eye the first time. It is unrealistic to expect to be on target immediately. You have to "fail" a number of times to succeed. By "failing,"

Don't let failure discourage you. Failure is part of the process of achieving success.

you discover ways that don't work. You go step by step toward the way that does work. This is how you aim for excellence.

Your Magic Sword

An old fable illustrates how confidence and failure work. A young knight wanted to be a hero by slaying the dragons that menaced his land. One day he found a sword that glowed strangely. He thought it was a magic sword, so he went out and killed a dragon with it. Everyone cheered him. Then the knight killed another dragon and was praised as a mighty warrior. He killed a third

Believing in yourself is half the battle in achieving a goal.

dragon, a fourth, a fifth, and so on. But then one day an old man told him that the sword was really a piece of scrap metal that had been thrown away by another knight years ago. That day the young knight went out to kill a dragon, but he never came back.

The power was not in the sword. The power was in himself. When he thought the sword had lost its magic, he lost his magic. The only magic involved was the magic he was manufacturing within himself.

The Magic Within You

Let's look at some people who realized that the magic was in themselves.

Demosthenes was an ancient Greek who had a speech defect. He knew that he had something important to tell the people. Day after day he went to the shore, stuffed pebbles in his mouth, and practiced speaking till he could make his voice heard clearly over the sound of the waves. Eventually he became a great Athenian statesman because he was such an eloquent speaker. He aimed at excellence and had confidence in himself.

Although he was partly deaf and had only three months of formal schooling, **Thomas Edison** became the greatest inventor of all time, patenting more than 1,000 inventions. He experimented thousands of times before he found the secret of the electric light. Even though people laughed at him, he knew that each "failure" was a step toward success. He knew he could create the incandescent bulb, and he did. Edison said, "Genius is 1 percent inspiration and 99 percent perspiration." He realized that he could not just wait for things to happen; he had to make them happen. He aimed at excellence and had confidence in himself.

At the age of two, **Helen Keller** had a serious illness that caused her to become blind, deaf, and unable to speak. Almost everyone thought she would go through life never being able to communicate. But her teacher, Anne Sullivan, never gave up. Eventually Helen learned to read, speak, and write. She became a highly educated woman who wrote many books and helped others who seemed beyond help. Her motto was, "The only way out is through," meaning that you cannot solve problems by running away from them. You have to deal with them head-on. Helen Keller and Anne Sullivan both aimed at excellence and had confidence in themselves and in each other.

Greg Louganis was diagnosed as dyslexic, was put up for adoption, felt unwanted and unloved, realized that he was gay, and abandoned himself to drugs and alcohol. But eventually he turned his life around and became such a skilled diver that he competed at the Olympic Games twice and was known as "The World's Greatest Diver." An example of his confidence occurred when he scraped his scalp on the edge of a diving board when performing during the Olympics. He had seen another diver die in a similar incident. But he simply had his scalp stitched and bandaged, got back on the diving board, and made a gold-medal dive. Later, no longer afraid of what people would think of him, he came out publicly and stated that he had AIDS. He helped raise money for AIDS research. He aimed at excellence and had confidence in himself.

These are people just like you. If they can build up their own confidence, so can you.

Many people can help you to build your self-confidence.

Fear and Excitement

When you feel fear, you are experiencing a strong emotion that has powerful effects on your body. The same is true when you feel excitement. Most people consider fear and excitement very different experiences. But when you aim for excellence, you know that they are often the same thing.

Let's see how Malcolm and Corinne deal with what they used to call fear.

When Malcolm thinks about swimming or goes to swim practice, he now tells himself, "Just do it, man!" He imagines himself swimming like a dolphin with the whole team cheering him on. When he wins a race, he thinks, "I knew I could do it!" When he

Failure does not mean you are defeated. Remember that
even walking was once a challenge.

doesn't win, he tells himself, "No problem. I'll do it next time." His fear is gone. He is confident in himself.

As Corinne works on her speech, she relaxes and focuses on a mental movie of herself speaking in front of the school board and all the students. She tells herself, "I will give the best speech I have ever given and convince the board to fund the music and art program." If she does make a mistake, she tells herself, "Take a breath and relax. Just go on with the speech." She is eager to make this the best speech ever instead of afraid to give it at all.

Situations that used to cause fear now create excitement. Why? Not because the situations have changed, but because Malcolm and Corinne are *doing* and *thinking* differently.

Be Patient with Yourself!

Creating confidence is a lifelong, full-time project. It's exciting to discover who you are and what you are capable of doing. Don't think that you are alone in your self-building project. Many people can help you— your family, friends, teachers, and fellow workers.

You have nothing to lose but your old negative thinking. You will gain more of who you really are.

Have patience with yourself. Even though you are not perfect, you can be excellent. You are a valuable human being who is in the process of becoming everything you are meant to be.

Glossary

alienate To cause a person to become unfriendly or hostile.

caution Forethought and prudence to reduce the risk of danger.

erroneous Mistaken; containing errors.

focus To concentrate one's attention upon an object or subject.

impoverished Poor; deprived of strength or wealth.

judgmental Having a tendency to judge harshly.

prophecy A prediction of something to come.

sabotage An act or process designed to hurt or hamper.

Where to Go for Help

You can talk about building your confidence with any responsible adult whom you trust. You might want to try a family member, a teacher, a social worker, your family doctor, or your family minister, priest, or rabbi.

If you don't feel comfortable with any of these people, look in the yellow pages of your telephone book or check your local newspaper under these listings:

Clergy
Counseling, Personal and Family
Health Department and Mental Health Clinics
Human Services Organizations
Mental Health Centers
Physicians and Surgeons
Psychologists
Self-Help Groups
Social Services Organizations
Social Workers
Youth Organizations and Centers

You can also write or call the following organizations for further assistance:

In the United States:

American Self-Help Clearinghouse
Saint Clare's Hospital
25 Pocono Road
Denville, NJ 07834
(973) 625-9565

Big Brothers/Big Sisters of America
230 North 13th Street
Philadelphia, PA 19107
(215) 567-7000

Boys and Girls Clubs of America
1230 West Peachtree Street NW
Atlanta, GA 30309
(404) 815-5700

National Mental Health Association
1021 Prince Street
Alexandria, VA 22314-2971
(703) 684-7722
(800) 433-5959

National Self-Help Clearinghouse
Center for Advanced Studies in Education (CASE)
33 West 42nd Street
New York, NY 10036
(212) 642-2944

New York City Self-Help Center
120 West 57th Street
New York, NY 10019
(212) 586-5770

In Canada:

The Self-Help Resource Centre of Greater Toronto
40 Orchard View Boulevard, Suite 219
Toronto, Ontario M4R 1B9
(416) 487-4355

For Further Reading

Berent, Jonathan, and Amy Lemley. *Beyond Shyness: How to Conquer Social Anxieties*. New York: Simon & Schuster, 1994.

Branden, Nathaniel. *Self-Esteem Every Day: Reflections on Self-Esteem and Spirituality*. New York: Simon & Schuster, 1998.

Carducci, Bernardo J., and Susan K. Golant. *Shyness: A Bold New Approach*. New York: HarperCollins, 1999.

Dyer, Wayne W. *Manifest Your Destiny*. New York: HarperCollins, 1997.

Feller, Robyn M. *Everything You Need to Know About Peer Pressure*. Rev. ed. New York: Rosen Publishing Group, 1997.

Frankl, Viktor. *Man's Search for Meaning*. New York: Pocket Books, 1963.

Goulston, Mark, and Philip Goldberg. *Get Out of Your Own Way: Overcoming Self-Defeating Behavior*. New York: Berkley Publishing Group, 1996.

Lowndes, Leil. *Talking the Winner's Way*. Chicago: NTC, Contemporary Publishing Co., 1999.

Warner, Mark J. *The Complete Idiot's Guide to Enhancing Self-Esteem*. New York: Macmillan, 1999.

Index

About the Author

Matthew Ignoffo teaches college-prep and graduate-level courses. He has written many articles and several books. He has master's and doctoral degrees in English, American Literature, and reading improvement from Loyola University of Chicago, Northwestern University, and Monmouth College. He is certified in neurolinguistics, hypnotherapy, and reality therapy. In addition to teaching and writing, he counsels people about self-improvement.

Photo Credits

Cover photo by Michael Brandt; pp. 17, 19, 21, 25 by Kim Sonsky; pp. 14, 30 by Katie McClancy; pp. 53, 56 by Michael Brandt; pp. 52, 57 by Lauren Piperno; p. 2 by Katherine Hsu; all other photos by Yung-Hee Chia.